NEUROSCIENCE, BELIEF SYSTEMS, AND OFFICER INVOLVED SHOOTINGS

WRITTEN BY DR. JOHN "JAY" HALL

ACKNOWLEDGEMENT

AS ONE JOURNEYS THROUGH LIFE, THERE ARE SO MANY PEOPLE WHO CROSS YOUR PATHS THAT INFLUENCE HOW YOU THINK AND SEE THE WORLD. THIS INCLUDES THE GOOD AND THE BAD, BECAUSE WE LEARN FROM EACH OTHER. AS WITH ANY OF MY WORK, I ALWAYS WANT TO THANK GOD AND MY PARENTS AND GRANDMOTHER, WHO DIDN'T HAVE MUCH BUT GAVE US A FOUNDATION RICH IN CHARACTER AND A LOT OF "YES, YOU CAN".

IN ADDITION TO MY IMMEDIATE FAMILY, I WOULD LIKE TO THANK MY SOUL MATE, COCO, FOR ALWAYS CHEERING ME UP WHEN I AM DOWN. MY DAUGHTER, JAMES, SR., JAYDA, JAYLA, AND JAMES, JR. MY THREE ACADEMY SISTERS, WHO ALWAYS HAD WORDS OF WISDOM: DR. JONELLA BRADFORD, DR. PAMELA WEBB-REDRICK, AND DR. MELANIE SMITH.

I WOULD ALSO LIKE TO THANK, CAPTAIN ROY RICE OF THE GARY POLICE DEPARTMENT WHO UNDERSTOOD THAT I WAS GOOD KID, GROWING UP IN A TOUGH NEIGHBORHOOD. I ALSO WANT TO THANK COLLEGE RECRUITER RUBEN RODRIGUEZ WHO WAS RESPONSIBLE FOR GETTING ME INTO CALUMET COLLEGE ON AN ACADEMIC SCHOLARSHIP. I ALSO WANT TO THANK OLGA AND NICK CIMESA, WHO OWNED THE NEIGHBORHOOD CORNER STORE AND LET US WORK AND EAT TO KEEP US OUT OF TROUBLE.

PRESENTLY, I LIKE TO THANK SOME NEW FRIENDS WHO SUPPORT THE WORK THAT I AM ATTEMPTING IN NEUROSCIENCE: SERGEANT NINO HICKS, OFFICER STAN MASON, ACTIVIST TY DUNMORE, TONY CRUSH, AND TIM. IF I MISS SOMEONE, MY APOLOGY. AGAIN, THANK EACH OF YOU FOR YOUR SUPPORT, IT HAS TRULY BEEN OF VALUE AND I WILL CONTINUE TO BE THE BEST VERSION OF WHOM I AM CAPABLE OF.

TABLE OF CONTENT

1 CORINTHIANS 12:22

There are diversities of gifts, but the same spirit, there are differences of administration, but the same spirit, there are diversities of operations, but the same God. The manifestation of the Spirit is given to every man to profit withal. Wisdom, gifts of healing, prophecy, discernment, speaking in tongues, interpreting tongues, all come from the same spirit. The eyes, the ears, the arm, the foot, are separate; yet all part of the body. There should be no schism in the body; all members should have the same care for one another. If one member suffers, all members suffer with it.

PROBLEM STATEMENT:

IN POLICE TRAINING, THERE SHOULD BE NO SCHISM BETWEEN THE TRAINING CONSTRUCTED FROM THE LEFT BRAIN AND TRAINING CONSTRUCTED FROM THE RIGHT BRAIN. CURRENT DE-ESCALATION TRAINING FOCUSES PRIMARILY ON POLICY AND PROCEDURES THAT ORGINATE FROM THE LEFT BRAIN. AS A RESULT OF THIS OVER EMPHASIS ON PROCEDURES AND SEQUENTIAL STEPS, THIS AUTHOR BELIEVES POLICE SHOOTING WILL CONTINUE UNLESS WE FOCUS OUR ATTENTION ON WHAT POLICE OFFICERS ARE SAYING AFTER AN OFFICER INVOLVED SHOOTING. IN MOST INSTANCES, THEY SAY, "I WAS IN FEAR OF MY LIFE".

WHILE THERE HAS BEEN A DISPROPORTIONAL NUMBER OF POLICE SHOOTINGS OF MINORITIES; POLICE HAVE ALSO SHOT AN EQUAL NUMBER OF WHITES BUT WHEN POPULATION ADJUSTMENTS ARE MADE, BLACKS AND BROWNS ARE SHOT DISPROPORTIONALLY MORE. UNDOUBTABLY, FEAR IS A FACTOR IN THE MAJORITY OF POLICE SHOOTING. FEAR IS PART OF OUR NATURAL EARLY WARNING SYSTEM; HOWEVER, IT BECOMES PROBLEMATIC IN POLICE WORK WHEN RACE BECOMES A FACTOR AND/OR WHEN FEAR BECOMES

UNMANAGEABLE. AS A BONIFIDED OCCUPATIONAL QUALIFIER, OFFICERS MUST BE ABLE TO MANAGE THEIR FEARS WHILE PRIORITIZING THE SANCTITY OF HUMAN LIFE. HEAVY WEIGHT BOXER, MIKE TYSON, SUMMARIZES WHAT THIS AUTHOR IS SAYING ABOUT FEAR WHEN HE STATED THAT *WHEN YOU GET IN THE RING WITH ME, YOU MIGHT HAVE A PLAN, BUT ONCE I HIT YOU, YOU WILL FORGET IT".* IRON MIKE, WASN'T A NEUROSCIENTIST, BUT HE UNDERSTOOD HUMAN NATURE.

HISTORY OF POLICE TRAINING:

IN 1967, THE PRESIDENTS COMMISION ON LAW ENFORCEMENT AND ADMINISTRATION OF JUSTICE DETERMINED THAT THERE WAS A GREATER NEED TO TRAIN THE POLICE. IT RECOMMENDED AT LEAST 400 HOURS OF INSTRUCTION AND A 12 TO 18 MONTH PROBATIONARY PERIOD. FROM AN EDUCATION POINT OF VIEW, AUGUST VOLLMER, BERKELEY, CALIFORNIA, FIRST POLICE CHIEF CLAIMED THAT THE MORE EDUCATED A POLICEMAN IS; THEN, THE MORE CAPABLE IS HE ABLE TO DEAL WITH THE STREET. BASED ON NUMEROUS LAWSUITS, THERE IS AN ESTABLISHED LINK BETWEEN POLICE TRAINING AND MUNICIPAL LIABILITY (HAWKES, JUNE 25, 2013). COMMUNITY POLICING BEGIN IN ENGLAND AND WAS REFERRED TO AS THE FRANKPLEDGE SYSTEM. MEN WITHIN THEIR COMMUNITIES WOULD FORM GROUPS OF TEN CALLED TYTHINGS. A HUNDRED OF THESE MEN WERE CALLED SHIRE REEVE, (SHERIFF), (POTTER, (2013). THESE GROUPS LATER CAME UNDER THE AUTHORITY OF THE LOCAL GOVERNMENT.

POLICING AND RACE RELATIONS:

IN TERMS OF AMERICAN RACIAL HISTORY, SOUTHERN WHITE COMMUNITY MEMBERS WERE ASSEMBLED TO DEVELOP SLAVE PATROLS. THIS FORM OF POLICING WAS USED TO INTIMIDATE AND TO LOCATE FUGITIVE SLAVES WHO RESISTED THEIR PLIGHT. ACCORDING TO REICHEL (1992), SLAVES WERE NOT ALWAYS VIEWED AS DOCILE AND HAPPY. MANY WHITES FEARED SLAVES BECAUSE SOME RESISTED THEIR PLIGHT BY REVOLTING.

GIVEN THE HISTORICAL CONTEXT, THE RELATIONSHIPS BETWEEN WHITES AND BLACKS THEN AND NOW CONTINUES TO BE LADENED WITH CULTURAL BAGGAGE. SO HOW DOES THIS RELATE TO POLICE TRAINING? AS THE ABOVE AUTHOR STATED, SLAVE PATROLS WERE PART OF THE ANTEBELLUM SOUTH'S POLICE FORCE, MANY OF THE PARTICIPANTS VIEWED SLAVE PATROLS AND ENFORCING THE SLAVE CODES AS THEIR CIVIC DUTY, FOR PAY, FOR REWARDS, OR BEING EXEMPT FOR MILITARY DUTY (REICHEL, 1992).

BEHAVIORAL MODIFICATION: A CRITIQUE

IN LAW ENFORCEMENT, THERE ARE SOME PARALLELS BETWEEN HOW WE USED BEHAVIORAL MODIFICATION TECHNIQUES TO CHANGE THE BEHAVIOR OF SLAVES AND HOW WE USED THE SAME PRINCIPLES TO CHANGE THE BEHAVIOR OF CRIMINALS. WITHIN LAW ENFORCEMENT, WE TEND TO MODIFY BEHAVIOR BY USING A MIXTURE OF LEARNING REINFORCERS THAT CONSIST OF REWARDS, PUNISHMENTS, AND EXTINCTIONS.

IRRESPECTIVE OF THE LEARNING REINFORCER USED, THE FOCUS OF THE STRATEGY (REWARD OR PUNISHMENT) WAS AIMED AT CONTROLLING AND CHANGING THE INDIVIDUAL'S BEHAVIOR AT THE EXPENSE OF IGNORING THE CONDITIONS UNDER WHICH THE INDIVIDUAL LIVED. IN ORDER TO ACHIEVE CONTROL, REWARDS AND PUNISHMENTS WERE APPLIED INDISCRIMINATELY TO INTIMIDATE AND INVOKE FEAR. THE NEXUS BETWEEN THE SLAVE PATROLS AND SOME CONTEMPORARY CRIMINAL JUSTICE PRACTICES JETTISONS ACROSS TIME PERIODS TO REOPEN "HARD WIRED" EPISODIC MEMORIES PASSED ON FROM ONE GENERATION TO THE NEXT. THESE MEMORIES CARRIED MESSAGES OF EMOTIONAL TRAUMA, FEAR, AND DISTRUST.

AND DESPITE, AN INCIDENT HAPPENING YEARS AGO, OUR BRAIN AND LONG TERM MEMORY RECORDED THE INCIDENT AS A FORM OF EMOTIONAL TRAUMA. TODAY, WE WANT TO RE-EXAMINE THE RELATIONSHIP OF USING REWARDS AND PUNISHMENTS AS A FORM OF OPERANT CONDITIONING THAT MAY REINFORCE AND CONTRIBUTE TO QUESTIONABLE POLICE SHOOTING BEHAVIORS. OPERANT CONDITIONING IS CONSIDERED SECOND TIER BEHAVIORAL CONDITIONING. THE FIRST FORM OF CONDITIONING WAS DEFINED AS CLASSIC CONDITIONING UNDER THE RESEARCH OF PAVLOC IN HIS EXPERIMENTATION WITH ANIMALS.

BASICALLY, PAVLOC'S THEORIZED THAT BY PAIRING A NEUTRAL OBJECT WITH AN EVENT THAT HAD A CAUSE AND EFFECT RELATIONSHIP; THEN, THE SAME RESULTS COULD BE ACHIEVED BY INTRODUCING A NEUTRAL OBJECT BY ITSELF AFTER ESTABLISHING AN **ASSOCIATION** WHICH WOULD DUPLICATE THE ORIGINAL CAUSE AND EFFECT RELATIONSHIP. FOR PURPOSES OF CLARITY, I AM INTERCHANGING THE STIMULUS RESPONSE BEHAVIOR MODEL WITH THE CAUSE AND EFFECT TERMINOLOGY BECAUSE EACH REPRESENT A FORM OF SINGLE LOOP LEARNING WHERE THE RULES, PROCEDURES, AND POLICIES ARE TAKEN FOR GRANTED WITHOUT CONSIDERING A NEED FOR REVISION.

FROM THEIR TRAINING IN THE POLICE ACADEMIES, POLICE ARE TAUGHT THE STIMULUS RESPONSE SHOOTER TRAINING TECHNIQUE. THIS PROCESS CONSIST OF FOCUSING ON A POTENTIALLY THREATENING TARGET, POINTING AT THE TARGET, AND SHOOTING THE TARGET. OVER YEARS OF PRACTICE, THIS TRAINING BECOMES "HARD WIRED" INTO A POLICE OFFICER'S NEURAL CIRCUITRY. IN ORDER TO UNDERSTAND HOW RACE, STEREOTYPES, AND FEAR BECOME FACTORS IN THE NARRATIVE ON POLICE SHOOTING, WE MUST FIRST UNDERSTAND THAT OUR BRAIN OPERATES ON PATTERN RECOGNITION AND ANY CHANGE IN OUR PATTERN AS WE PERCEIVED IT IS A "THREAT" TO WHAT WE CONSIDER ROUTINE OR NORMAL.

IN ORDER TO BEGIN TO DE-CONSTRUCT OUR PAST LEARNING, PROGRAMMING, ASSUMPTIONS, AND BELIEFS THAT MAY ADVERSELY IMPACT POLICE SHOOTING TECHNIQUES, NEUROSCIENCE CAN SERVE A CRITICAL ROLE IN CONTRIBUTING TO OUR UNDERSTANDING OF HOW THE BRAIN OPERATES ON THE **PRINCIPLE OF ASSOCIATION** BY COMPARING OUR PAST EXPERIENCES WITH PEOPLE TO OUR PRESENT ONES.

TO SHOW HOW ASSOCIATIONS ARE REINFORCED, THE AUTHOR WILL PROVIDE THREE TYPES OF CONDITIONING AT THREE LEVELS THAT MAY CONTRIBUTE TO QUESTIONABLE POLICE SHOOTINGS. IN ADDITION, THE AUTHOR PROVIDED THE EXISTING DEFINITION OF THE USE OF FORCE LAW, A THEORY ON EMOTIONS, AND THE DIAGRAM ILLUSTRATING THE THREE TIERS OF LEARNING WHICH ARE CLASSICAL CONDITIONING, OPERANT CONDITIONING, AND OBERVATION LEARNING OR SOCIAL LEARNING. NEXT, THE AUTHOR ALSO PROVIDES A LIST OF SUGGESTIONS/QUESTIONS TO REDUCE POLICE SHOOTINGS AND PROPOSES THAT NEUROSCIENCE BE USED AS A LEARNING INTERVENTION. FINALLY, THE AUTHOR ADDS SOME CONCLUDING REMARKS. BELOW, WE START WITH THE DEFINITION OF THE INDUSTRY'S LEGAL STANDARD FOR THE USE OF FORCE.

LEGAL USE OF FORCE DEFINITION

USE OF DEADLY FORCE

1. AN OFFICER IS AUTHORIZED TO USE DEADLY FORCE WHEN IT IS **OBJECTIVELY   REASONABLE UNDER THE TOTALITY OF THE CIRCUMSTANCES**. USE OF DEADLY FORCE IS JUSTIFIED WHEN ONE OR BOTH OF THE FOLLOWING APPLY: A. TO PROTECT THE OFFICER OR OTHERS FROM WHAT IS **REASONABLY BELIEVED TO BE AN IMMEDIATE THREAT OF DEATH OR SERIOUS BODILY INJURY.** B. TO PREVENT THE ESCAPE OF A FLEEING SUBJECT WHEN THE OFFICER HAS PROBABLE CAUSE TO BELIEVE THAT THE PERSON HAS COMMITTED, OR INTENDS TO COMMIT A FELONY INVOLVING SERIOUS BODILY INJURY OR DEATH, AND THE OFFICER REASONABLY BELIEVES THAT THERE IS AN IMMINENT RISK OF SERIOUS BODILY INJURY OR DEATH TO THE OFFICER OR ANOTHER IF THE SUBJECT IS NOT IMMEDIATELY APPREHENDED.

2. WHERE FEASIBLE, THE OFFICER SHALL IDENTIFY HIMSELF OR HERSELF AS A LAW ENFORCEMENT OFFICER AND WARN OF HIS OR HER INTENT TO USE DEADLY FORCE.

3. DEADLY FORCE RESTRICTIONS

a. DEADLY FORCE SHOULD NOT BE USED AGAINST PERSONS WHOSE ACTIONS ARE A THREAT ONLY TO THEMSELVES OR PROPERTY.

b. WARNING SHOTS ARE INHERENTLY DANGEROUS. THEREFORE, A WARNING SHOT MUST HAVE A DEFINED TARGET AND SHALL NOT BE FIRED UNLESS (1) THE USE OF DEADLY FORCE IS JUSTIFIED (2) THE WARNING SHOT WILL NOT POSE A SUBSTANTIAL RISK OF INJURY OR DEATH TO THE OFFICER OR OTHERS; AND (3) THE OFFICER REASONABLY BELIEVES THAT THE WARNING SHOT WILL REDUCE THE POSSIBILITY THAT DEADLY FORCE WILL HAVE TO BE USED.

c. FIREARMS SHALL NOT BE DISCHARGED AT A MOVING VEHICLE UNLESS (1) A PERSON IN THE VEHICLE IS THREATENING THE OFFICER OR ANOTHER PERSON

WITH DEADELY FORCE BY MEANS OTHER THAN THE VEHICLE; OR (2) THE VEHICLE IS OPERATED IN A MANNER DELIBERATELY INTENDED TO STRIKE THE OFFICER OR ANOTHER PERSON, AND ALL OTHER REASONABLE MEANS OF DEFENSE HAVE BEEN EXHAUSTED (OR ARE NOT PRESENT OR PRACTICAL), WHICH INCLUDES MOVING OUT OF THE PATH OF THE VEHICLE.

d. FIREARMS SHALL NOT BE DISCHARGED FROM A MOVING VEHICLE EXCEPT IN EXIGENT CIRCUMSTANCES. IN THESE SITUATIONS, AN OFFICER MUST HAVE AN ARTICULABLE REASON FOR THIS USE OF DEADLY FORCE.

e. CHOKE HOLDS ARE PROHIBITED UNLESS DEADLY FORCE IS AUTHORIZED.

4 E. TRAINING. 1. **ALL OFFICERS SHALL RECEIVE TRAINING, AT LEAST ANNUALLY**, ON THIS AGENCY'S USE OF FORCE POLICY AND RELATED LEGAL UPDATES. 2. IN ADDITION, TRAINING SHALL BE PROVIDED ON A REGULAR AND PERIODIC BASIS AND DESIGNED TO A. PROVIDE TECHNIQUES FOR THE USE OF FORCE OF AND REINFORCE THE IMPORTANCE OF DE-ESCALATION; B. SIMULATE ACTUAL SHOOTING SITUATIONS AND CONDITIONS; AND C. ENHANCE OFFICERS' DISCRETION AND JUDGMENT IN USING LESS LETHAL AND DEADLY FORCE IN ACCORDANCE WITH THIS POLICY. 3. ALL USE OF FORCE TRAINING SHALL BE DOCUMENTED. **TENNESSEE V. GARNER 471 U.S. 1 (1985)** SOURCE: NATIONAL CONSENSUS POLICY ON USE OF FORCE (JANUARY 2017).

POLICE SHOOTING AND EXCESSIVE FORCE INCIDENTS ARE EXPLAINED USING THE STANDARD OF **"OBJECTIVE REASONABLENESS"**. THIS STANDARD IMPLIES THAT POLICE SHOOTING AND EXCESSIVE FORCE CASES BE EVALUATED BASED ON THE WORLD VIEW AND THE ACTIONS MOST LIKELY TAKEN BY OTHER POLICE OFFICERS IN SIMILAR CIRCUMSTANCES. **GRAHAM V. CONNER (1989).**

WITH RESPECT TO THE ABOVE LAWS AND POLICIES, MOST POLICE DEPARTMENTS ARE AWARE OF THE NEED TO COLLECT REVELANT FORMS OF USE OF FORCE AND DE-ESCALATION DATA TO IMPROVE EXISTING TRAINING PRACTICES. IN THE NEXT SECTION, THE AUTHOR FOCUSES ON THE MOST IMPORTANT COMPONENT OF ANY TRAINING THE PARTICIPANTS. IN THE SECTION BELOW, THE AUTHOR PROVIDES A THEORY THAT HELPS EXPLAIN AN OFFICER'S BELIEF SYSTEM. AND HOW THEIR ASSOCIATIONS CAN INFLUENCE THEIR DECISION MAKING.

THE A-B-C THEORY OF EMOTIONS

ACCORDING TO DR. ALBERT ELLIS (1991a), A RENOWED PSYCHOLOGIST, OUR EMOTIONAL REACTION TO AN EVENT IS NOT REALLY ABOUT THE EVENT BUT ABOUT **OUR BELIEFS** ABOUT THAT EVENT. THIS IS A CRUCIAL PIECE OF INFORMATION WHEN HEARING STATEMENTS SUCH AS "I WAS IN FEAR OF MY LIFE". IN HIS MODEL, DR. ELLIS STATED THAT THE **A** REPRESENTS THE ACTIVATING EVENT, STIMULUS, OR CAUSE, AND **B** REPRESENTS OUR **BELIEF SYSTEM OR FEELINGS**. AND FINALLY, DR. ELLIS STATED THAT **C** REPRESENTS THE CONSEQUENCES OR THE EMOTION(S) THAT WE CHOSE TO PAIR OUR BELIEF(S) WITH. ELLIS BELIEVED THAT OUR BELIEFS INFLUENCED HOW WE PROCESS OUR EXPERIENCES.

IN POLICING, ELLIS'S THEORY REJECTS THE NOTION THAT ALL TRAINING FITS ALL OFFICERS AND SUPPORTS THE NOTION THAT TWO POLICE OFFICERS DUE TO THEIR BELIEF SYSTEMS CAN PROCESS THE SAME INFORMATION DIFFERENTLY. SINCE HIS ORIGINAL MODEL, ELLIS ADDED TWO OTHER COMPONENTS OF THE MODEL, WHERE **D** REPRESENTED DISPUTING ONE'S ORIGINAL BELIEFS AND **E** REPRESENTED A NEW EFFECT OR NEW BEHAVIOR (ELLIS, 1991b).

BASED ON THE ORIGINAL MODEL, THE EVENT OF SEEING A BLACK MAN ON A CALL FOR SERVICE IS NOT THE PROBLEM. THE PROBLEM IS WHAT STEROTYPICAL BELIEFS THAT THE OFFICER HOLDS ABOUT A BLACK MAN OR A BROWN MAN. **THE QUESTION REALLY BECOMES WHAT SET OF EMOTIONS**

DOES THE OFFICER DECIDE TO MATCH WITH HIS OR HER BELIEF SYSTEM?

THIS EXAMPLE REPRESENTS THE GENERAL THEORY BUT IN REAL LIFE IT BECOMES MORE COMPLICATED A) WHEN WE HAVE NO KNOWLEDGE OF THE OFFICER'S BELIEF SYSTEM, B) WHEN WE ATTEMPT TO REVIEW AN OFFICER'S BELIEF SYSTEM AFTER A SHOOTING OCCURS, AND C) WHEN CURRENT METHODS DO NOT SCIENTIFICALLY TEST, ASSESS, AND MEASURE AN OFFICER'S BELIEF SYSTEM.

THE LACK OF KNOWLEDGE ABOUT AN OFFICER'S BELIEF SYSTEM CAUSES THE COMMUNITY TO QUESTION THE OFFICER'S ACTIONS; BUT, MORE IMPORTANTLY, CAUSES THE COMMUNITY TO QUESTION THE OFFICER'S INTENTIONS. NEUROSCIENCE CAN ALLEVIATE SOME OF THESE CONCERNS WHEN USED AS AN ASSESSMENT TOOL IN READING BRAIN ACTIVITY THAT DEAL WITH AREAS SUCH AS FEAR ASSOCIATIONS, RACIAL ATTITUDES, AND STEREOTYPIC VIEWS AS PART OF A RECRUITMENT SCREENING PROCESS.

BASED ON CURRENT RESEARCH, WE KNOW THAT FEAR AND STRESS CONTRIBUTE TO PERCEPTUAL ERRORS IN ASSESSING THE ENVIRONMENT OR THE CONTEXTUAL FRAMEWORK THAT AN OFFICER IS OPERATING IN; YET, WE KNOW LITTLE ABOUT HOW INDIVIDUAL OFFICERS ARE AFFECTED AND HOW THEIR PERFORMANCE IS AFFECTED.

IN AN EFFORT TO BETTER UNDERSTAND HOW AN OFFICER'S BELIEF SYSTEM, ASSOCIATIONS, AND TRAINING CAN POSSIBLE INFLUENCE POLICE SHOOTING OUTCOMES, THE AUTHOR HIGHLIGHTS THREE CLOSELY RELATED FORMS OF LEARNING THAT MAY INFLUENCE OFFICER INVOLVED SHOOTINGS. **SEE THE DIAGRAM BELOW:**

THREE LEVELS OF CONDITIONING OR PROGRAMMING IMPACTING OFFICER INVOLVED SHOOTINGS:

DIAGRAM: THREE LEVELS OF CONDITIONING OR PROGRAMMING IMPACTING OFFICER INVOLVED SHOOTINGS:

LEVEL 1: CLASSICAL CONDITIONING

FOCUS: INDIVIDUAL POLICE OFFICER'S BELIEF SYSTEM

STIMULUS/RESPONSE/ASSOCIATIONS/PAIRING

FILTERS:

a) Past experiences
b) Emotional histories
c) Explicit racial bias/ implicit bias
d) Stereotypic views
e) Post-traumatic stress incidents
f) Fear threshold
g) Social polarization

SHOOT INCENTIVE

SURVIVAL

RIGHT BRAIN

PROCEDURAL MEMORY

STARTLED REFLEX

SHOOT DISINCENTIVE

NON-THREATENED

LEFT/RIGHT BRAIN

PROPER TRAINING

PROPER RECRUITING

LEVEL 2: OPERANT CONDITIONING

FOCUS: POLICE ADMINISTRATION AND COMMUNITY

THIRD PARTY SELECTS REWARDS AND

PUNISHMENTS TO REINFORCE OR

EXTINGUISH OFFICER'S BEHAVIOR

SHOOT INCENTIVE

SAVE OFFICER/CITIZEN LIFE

DIRTY HARRY MENTALITY

NO COMPLAINT PENALTY/ UNIONS

POLICE CODE OF SILENCE

IGNORING SYSTEMIC CONDITIONS

SHOOT DISINCENTIVE

SAVE SUSPECT LIVE

PROTECT CIVIL LIBERTIES OF SUSPECT

BUILD COMMUNITY TRUST

IMPROVE POLICE COMM. RELATIONS

LEVEL 3: OBSERVATION LEARNING/SOCIAL LEARNING THEORY

FOCUS: SUPREME COURT

PUBLIC SENTIMENT

GROUP SENSE MAKING

SHOOT INCENTIVE

FEW CRIMINAL CONVICTIONS OIS

LAW FAVORS PERCEPTION OF OFFICER

SHOOT DISINCENTIVE

A PLAN TO ERADICATE SYSTEMIC CONDITIONS

A PLAN TO ERADICATE SCHOOL TO PRISON PIPELINE

SOURCE: DR. JOHN "JAY" HALL/ 4-12-18

**HOW CAN A NEUROSCIENCE COURSE AND A NEUROSCIENCE ASSESSMENT
TOOL REDUCE POLICE SHOOTING?**

IN THIS NEXT TO THE LAST SECTION, THE AUTHOR OFFERS SOME SUGGESTIONS
ON HOW AND WHY NEUROSCIENCE CAN BE USEFUL AS A POLICE ACADEMY
COURSE AND AS AN ASSESSMENT TOOL IN REDUCING OFFICER INVOLVED
SHOOTINGS. BASED ON THE RESEARCH SHARED BY ELLIS, CHANGING AN
OFFICER'S BEHAVIOR MAY REQUIRE US TO BEGIN BY DETECTING AND
CORRECTING ERRORS IN AN OFFICER'S BELIEF SYSTEM. THIS AUTHOR BELIEVES
FOCUSING ON AN OFFICER'S BELIEF SYSTEM IS CRITICAL IN UNDERSTANDING
HOW AN OFFICER SUBJECTIVELY PROCESSES CERTAIN PEOPLE, ETHNIC GROUPS,
 STEREOTYPES, NEIGHBORHOODS, AND THREATS IN ORDER TO CHANGE HIS OR
HER BEHAVIOR IF POSSIBLE. NEXT, POLICE ADMINISTRATORS MUST ASSESS
WHETHER OR NOT THE CURRENT TRAINING PROCESS CONTRIBUTES TO "FAULTY
HARD WIRING" THAT LEADS TO "UNANTICIPATED" CONSEQUENCES. IN AN
ATTEMPT TO ADDRESS THESE CONCERNS, THE FOLLOWING QUESTIONS WERE
FORMULATED:

HOW DO WE ASSESS WHETHER AN OFFICER'S BELIEF SYSTEM IS IN ALIGNMENT
WITH HUMANITARIAN NORMS AND VALUES?

HOW DO WE IDENTIFY INDIVIDUAL OFFICERS WITH LOW FEAR THESHOLDS?

HOW DO WE IDENTIFY INDIVIDUAL OFFICERS WITH RACIAL, STEREOTYPICAL
VIEWS, AND EMOTIONAL TRAUMA?

HOW DO WE IDENTIFY NEGATIVE LEARNING THAT MAY CONTRIBUTE TO
QUESTIONABLE POLICE SHOOTING AND EXCESSIVE USES OF FORCE?

HOW DO WE IDENTIFY POSITIVE LEARNING REINFORCERS THAT CONTRIBUTE TO THE REDUCTION OF QUESTIONABLE POLICE SHOOTING?

HOW DO WE ESTABLISH BEHAVIORAL PARAMETERS THAT REQUIRE MORE THAN THE OFFICER'S PERCEPTION OF AN IMMINENT THREAT OF BODILY HARM OR DEATH?

HOW CAN WE BE ENSURE THAT ALL INCIDENT REPORTS DOCUMENT WHY AN OFFICER SHOT OR DIDN'T SHOOT A SUSPECT **WILL BE RECORDED** IN ORDER TO EVALUATE EXISTING TRAINING METHODS AND TO DEVELOP A SET OF BEST PRACTICES?

HOW DO WE REVISE POLICE SHOOTING TECHNIQUES THAT REDUCE STARTLED REFLEX SHOOTING?

HOW DO WE ENSURE THAT POLICE TRAINING WITH RESPECT TO OFFICER INVOLVED SHOOTINGS ARE NOT COUNTERPRODUCTIVE IN TERMS OF "HARD WIRING" THE WRONG TECHNIQUES?

HOW DO WE GET THE COMMUNITY INVOLVED AS A PARTNER IN CO-DESIGNING AND CO-EVALUATING POLICE TRAINING?

HOW DO WE CREATE ALTERNATIVE SCENARIOS WHERE LIVES ARE SAVED AND THESE BEST PRACTICES BECOME "HARDWIRED"?

CONCLUSION:

THE SKEPTICISM ABOUT POLICE SHOOTINGS AND THE SKEPTICISM OF THE POLICE HELD BY THE BLACK AND BROWN COMMUNITIES ARE BASED ON PAST EXPERIENCES, NORMS, AND PRACTICES THAT HAVE BEEN "HARD WIRED". THIS AUTHOR BELIEVES THAT WHEN WE COMPARE THE INDUSTRY STANDARDS FOR USE OF FORCE TRAINING TO THE SYSTEMIC CONDITIONS AND CONDITIONING THAT HAVE INFLUENCE BOTH POLICE AND CITIZENS' ATTITUDES AND VIEWS ABOUT ONE ANOTHER; THEN, THE "HARD WIRING" RESULTING FROM THESE SYSTEMIC CONDITIONS CARRIED A STRONGER NEURAL SIGNAL. IN ORDER TO OFFSET YEARS OF "DEFERRED MAINTENANCE" OF THESE SYSTEMIC CONDITIONS, POLICE TRAINING MUST PROVIDE STRONGER POSITIVE REINFORCEMENT IN TERMS OF BOTH QUANTITY (AN INCREASE IN THE NUMBER OF DE-ESCALATION AND USE OF FORCE TRAINING HOURS) AND QUALITY (ALTERNATIVE POSITIVE REINFORCEMENT TRAINING THAT RESULTS IN DIFFERENT WAYS TO SAVE LIVES). THIS AUTHOR BELIEVES NEUROSCIENCE RESEARCH AND TRAINING CAN PLAY A PIVOTAL ROLE IN THIS ITERATIVE PROCESS.

IGNORING THE SYSTEMIC CONDITIONS THAT INFLUENCE POLICE AND CITIZENS' MINDSETS; **IS JUST NOT**, **SOUND LOGIC**, IF POLICE ADMINISTRATORS INTENT TO IMPROVE POLICE TRAINING AND IMPROVE POLICE COMMUNITY RELATIONS. UNDERSTANDING BOTH THE ASSUMPTIONS ASSOCIATED WITH POLICE TRAINING AND THE BELIEF SYSTEMS OF THE "BEST" OFFICERS HIRED ARE KEY SUCCESS FACTORS IN **DE-CONSTRUCTING PAST LEARNING** PRACTICES IN ORDER TO CONSTRUCT NEW ONES. NEUROSCIENCE CAN BE UTILIZED TO IMPROVE OFFICER INVOLVED SHOOTINGS BY SYNTHESIZING   INFORMATION GLEANED FROM BOTH LEFT AND RIGHT BRAIN RESEARCH.

WHILE THE USE OF FORCE TECHNIQUES AND TOOLS, SUCH AS
BATONS, TASERS, GUNS, BODY CAMS, AND SCENARIO SIMULATIONS ARE
BENEFICIAL, THE ONLY THING THAT SEPARATES A TRAINING SCENARIO FROM A
REAL LIFE SITUATION IS THE POLICEMAN'S JUDGEMENT. NEUROSCIENCE
OFFERS A DETECTION AND CORRECTION APPARATUS THAT MEASURES RACIAL
ATTITUDES, STEREOTYPICAL VIEWS, AND ACCEPTABLE FEAR LEVELS THAT
IMPACT JUDGEMENT AND DECISION MAKING. INCLUDING NEUROSCIENCE INTO
OUR POLICE TRAINING CURRICULUM ENHANCES OUR UNDERSTANDING OF THE
HUMAN BRAIN WHICH STILL REMAINS OUR GREATEST ASSET.

REFERENCES:

ELLIS, A. *(1991a).* THE ABC'S OF RET. THE HUMANIST, 51(1), 19-49.

ELLIS, A. *(1991b).* THE REVISED ABC'S OF RATIONAL EMOTIVE THERAPY. JOURNAL OF RATIONAL EMOTIVE AND COGNITIVE BEHAVIOR THERAPY, 9(3), 139-172.

GRAHAM V. CONNER (1989)

HAWKES, A. (JUNE, 2013). POLICELINK.MONSTER.

HTTPS://EN.WIKIPEDIA.ORG/WIKI/CLASSICAL RETRIEVED ON 4-12-18

NATIONAL CONSENSUS POLICY ON USE OF FORCE (JANUARY 2017).

POTTER, G. (JUNE, 2013). HISTORY OF POLICING IN THE UNITIED STATES, PART 1

PRESIDENT'S COMMISSION ON LAW ENFORCEMENT AND ADMINISTRATION OF JUSTICE (1967). THE CHALLENGE OF A FREE SOCIETY. WASHINGTON, D.C.

REICHEL, P. (1992). "THE MISPLACED EMPHASIS ON URBANIZATION ON POLICE DEVELOPMENT", POLICING AND SOCIETY 3 NO.1

TENNESSEE V. GARNER 471 U.S. 1 (1985)

ABOUT THE AUTHOR:

- DR. JOHN "JAY" HALL, IS A RETIRED LIEUTENANT THAT SERVED ON THE
-
- HOUSTON POLICE DEPARTMENT FOR TWENTY-THREE AND A HALF YEARS.
-
- DR. JAY IS ONE OF NINE CHILDREN, AND THE ONLY CHILD WHO ATTENDED
-
- A FOUR COLLEGE. HE GREW UP IN GARY, IND. – CHICAGO, ILL., AND
-
- DEVELOPED HIS GRIT FROM BEING ONE OF THE "CORNER BOYS". WITH
-
- SOME HELP FROM SOME DECENT COPS, WHO SAW HIS POTENTIAL, HE WAS
-
- ENCOURAGED TO GO TO COLLEGE. HIS ACADEMIC ACHIEVEMENTS: B.A.
-
- SOCIOLOGY AND CRIMINAL JUSTICE FROM ST. JOSEPH COLLEGE; M.A.
-
- PUBLIC ADMINISTRATION FROM INDIANA UNIVERSITY NW; M.S.M. IN
-
- MANAGEMENT FROM HOUSTON BAPTIST UNIVERSITY; AND A PHD IN
-
- ORGANIZATIONAL BEHAVIORAL AND MANAGEMENT, WITH A
-
- SPECIALIZATION IN LEADERSHIP FROM CAPELLA UNIVERSITY. DR. HALL
-
- DEDICATES ANY ACCOMPLISHMENTS TO HIS FATHER WHO ONLY OBTAINED
-
- A FOURTH GRADE EDUCATION, BUT HONORABLY SERVED IN THE MILITARY
-
- AS DID ALL HIS BROTHERS WITH THE EXCEPTION OF ONE. AS A BABY
-
- BLOOMER, HIS WORLD VIEW IS STILL INFLUENCED BY THE CIVIL RIGHTS
-
- STRUGGLE AND SOCIAL JUSTICE. HE BELIEVES IN TEACHING INDIVIDUALS

- HOW TO FISH RATHER THAN JUST GIVING THEM A FISH. ITS' PART OF HIS

- TOUGH LOVE CAMPAIGN FOR INDIVIDUAL GROWTH AND SOCIAL CHANGE.

- HIS FRIENDS CALL HIM JAY OR JOHN JAY.

WWW.DRJAYHALL.COM

EMAIL: JAYEARL2007@YAHOO.COM